Other titles by Jeffrey Kinghorn from

## RMJ DONALD, LLC
### Fine Books and Plays

Ted Mitchell Detective Novels
**Inside the Loop**
**The Cutter**
**1-800-Forgive**

For Families/Young Readers
**When We Were Happy**

Plays
**Shoulders**
**In A Coal-Burning House**

*Available worldwide*

# SOMETHING HAPPENED

Key:

        | | |
        |---|---|
        | EXT. | Exterior |
        | INT. | Interior |
        | (off) | Heard but not seen |
        | POV | Point of View |
        | V.O. | Voiceover (narration) |

FADE IN:

EXT. A RED DODGE RAM/MOVING — DAY

The pickup disappears down a peaceful, shade-dappled street.

EXT. DODGE RAM/MOVING – DAY

It weaves through heavy traffic as if charmed. We HEAR a tap on a microphone and a young girl's voice.

                    T.J. (V.O.)
          The title of my speech is Violence.

EXT. DODGE RAM/MOVING – DAY

It glides unhampered through a red light.

                    T.J. (V.O.)
               What is violence?

EXT. DODGE RAM/MOVING – DAY

It accelerates through a shopping center parking lot and plows through the front window of

RUBY'S RESTAURANT.

Its Texas Vanity License Plate reads: *RANDOM.*

                    T.J. (V.O.)
          I asked others what they thought it was.

INT. RUBY'S RESTAURANT — DAY

Glass and dust settle around the pickup as combat boots step down out of the cab.

                    T.J. (V.O.)
          I was surprised by the answers

They belong to a man in military fatigues who has an automatic weapon in each hand and a clutch of grenades at his waist.

EXT. PARKING LOT/SILENT — DAY

Patrons in the parking lot are unsure of what they've just witnessed.

Automatic gunfire erupts from inside, made visible in the shattering of what is left of the front windows.

                    T.J. (V.O.)
          My grandfather said: *Royal Oak.*

The patrons wait for more.

INT. RUBY'S RESTAURANT/SILENT — DAY

The soldier takes a grenade in each hand and settles cross-legged on the floor.

                    T.J. (V.O.)
          He was referring to a Post Office shooting
          in Michigan.

He pulls the pins with his teeth, spits them out, holds the grenades to his chest, and folds forward over his knees.

EXT. RUBY'S RESTAURANT/SILENT — DAY

The grenades blast debris into the parking lot. The patrons shake their heads in disgust and continue on their way.

Banal sounds creep back in—footsteps, car doors closing, a car horn, perhaps...even laughter.

INT. AUDITORIUM STAGE/PODIUM — DAY

T.J., a ten-year-old who avoids all things girlish speaks into the microphone.

                       T.J.
             It's called: *Going Postal.*

She drops her note cards which causes bursts of laughter from the audience. But she quickly regains her cool, picks up the cards, and sets them aside on the podium.

                       T.J.
            He used to be a mailman.

She takes the microphone off its stand and comes out from behind the podium.

                       T.J.
            For those who may not know, my
            grandmother teaches here.

EXT. SHOE STORE WINDOW — DAY

T.J. ogles a pair of athletic shoes on display, while her grandfather

STEPHEN INGERSOLL admires a pair of young girl's pumps.

>                    STEPHEN
>          See anything?

>                         T.J.
>     Yes.

>                    STEPHEN
>          We going in?

>                         T.J.
>     My birthday present, right?

>                    STEPHEN
>     Yes.

>                         T.J.
>     My choice, no argument?

>                    STEPHEN
>          That was the deal.

T.J. leads the way inside. Stephen follows.

EXT. SHOE STORE WINDOW — DAY

The athletic shoes are removed from the window display.

> T.J. (V.O.)
> She said violence could be anything.

INT.  CLASS ROOM – DAY

BARBARA INGERSOLL monitors a quiz. She retains the glamour that could have taken her far beyond a classroom.

> T.J. (V.O.)
> A war, an earthquake, a bad life-choice.

The DONAHUE TWINS wither at the back of the classroom under her scrutiny.

INT. INGERSOLL GARAGE – DAY

T.J.'s new athletic shoes stick out from under one side of a classic Ford Mustang.

Stephen's spit-shined black oxfords stick out from under the other side.

> STEPHEN (V.O.)
> Trick is to change it religiously.

INT. UNDER THE MUSTANG — DAY

T.J. loosens the nut on the oil pan under Stephen's watchful eye.

> STEPHEN
> It's the engine's blood system.

He sticks a finger in the oil flow.

>                    STEPHEN
>          Viscosity. Memorize it.

T.J. follows her grandfather's example.

INT. DENTAL OFFICE – DAY

HARRY MILLET *(MILL-it)* reclines in the chair. He is a Postman and is in uniform.

DARLENE HUNNICUT, the Assistant, attends on one side of the chair, as the

DENTIST, with drill in hand on the other side, dives into Harry's mouth.

>                  T.J. (V.O.)
>     I asked my mother who is a Dental Assistant.

INT. INGERSOLL KITCHEN – DAY

A pot of chocolate simmers on the stove. T.J. stirs. Stephen watches closely.

>                  T.J. (V.O.)
>          She said a root canal.

>                    STEPHEN
>          This recipe have a name?

T.J. dunks a waffle into the chocolate and lets the excess drain off.

>                      T.J.
>          Chocolate steak.

> STEPHEN
> What's the peanut butter for?

> T.J.
> Gravy.

T.J. sticks a finger into the chocolate flow.

Stephen follows her lead.

> T.J.
> Viscosity. Memorize it.

FULL SCREEN

Birthday cake with the icing-inscription:

HAPPY BIRTHDAY T.J.

Several pieces have been cut out of it.

REVEAL

INT. DINING ROOM/KITCHEN — NIGHT

Darlene clears the dining table to the kitchen where

Barbara scrapes and rinses plates and hands them to

T.J. who loads the dishwasher.

> DARLENE
> Dinner was brilliant, T.J.

                    BARBARA
Chocolate steak. Where have we been?

                    DARLENE
How'd you make the gravy?

                      T.J.
Peanut butter melted into Marshmallow
Fluff.

                  T.J. (V.O.)
I asked classmates what they thought
it was.

INT. DEN – NIGHT

Stephen polishes his black oxfords. A cooking show is on
the television, featuring

LEG of LAMB that is repeatedly skewered into which slits
are thrust garlic cloves.

                  T.J. (V.O.)
Most girls said: *Rape.*

T.J. bounces in and onto the couch next to Stephen.

                  STEPHEN
Homework.

                      T.J.
Birthday.

                  STEPHEN
Deal's a deal.

She drags herself out of the room.

                    T.J. (V.O.)
          Most boys said: *Stuff that goes fast and
          then blows up.*

INT. DINING ROOM — NIGHT

Barbara sits at the table grading papers.

Darlene sets down a photograph album and wrestles
into her coat.

                    DARLENE
          Might be late tonight.

                    BARBARA
          How late?

T.J. comes in still evading homework.

                    T.J.
          You going out again?

                    DARLENE
          Homework, young lady.

                    T.J.
          You have a boyfriend, don't you?

Barbara cocks an ear for Darlene's answer.

                    DARLENE
          It's my group night.

T.J. leafs through photo album.

BARBARA
Wouldn't I like to be a fly on that wall.

DARLENE
I doubt it.

T.J.
Why you taking your wedding album?

DARLENE
Day off from school, homework after
dinner, that was the deal.

T.J. drags herself out of the room.

BARBARA
I raised my children. I'm not interested
in raising yours.

DARLENE
I'll be home as soon as I can.

She makes a quick exit.

EXT. LAKE SPRINGFIELD/BEACH – NIGHT

WOMEN are gathered around a campfire. One of them
operates a VIDEO CAMERA and tapes a ceremony to
help recently divorced women get on with their lives.

T.J. (V.O.
There were six definitions in the dictionary.

VIDEO IMAGE

CONNIE holds up her WEDDING ALBUM.

                    CONNIE
        Heartache, heartbreak, and heartburn.

She pitches the album into the fire. The women whistle
and applaud.

                    T.J. (V.O.)
        Here are two. Intensity in natural
        phenomena, as in the violence of a
        hurricane.

VIDEO IMAGE

MARGARET, an athlete, hurls her wedding album into
the lake like a discus then turns back to the camera.

                    MARGARET
        I was drowning.

The women applaud.

                    T.J. (V.O.)
        Mother Nature can be a piece a work,
        that's for sure.

VIDEO IMAGE

REBECCA, no stranger to Goth, drives a wooden stake
through her wedding album.

The women applaud.

> T.J. (V.O.)
> Or a force exerted to damage, injure, or abuse.

VIDEO IMAGE

Darlene holds a shovel and her album

> DARLENE
> I was going to bury this. But I was a size six back then and this is my only proof.

Laughter and applause from the women.

> T.J. (V.O.)
> My grandmother was right. Violence can be anything, a thought, an action, a word, a decision, a choice, an event.

> DARLENE
> When Richard left, it felt like I might die.

> T.J. (V.O.)
> Purposeful, accidental, large or small.

> DARLENE
> I got the house and then had to sell it to pay off the credit cards I had maxed out.

> T.J. (V.O.)
> It can be quiet on the inside or explosive on the outside.

> DARLENE
> I made a career out of being invisible.

> **T.J. (V.O.)**
> We can even do violence to ourselves.

> **DARLENE**
> I'm glad now that he left because I never
> would have.

INT. STAGE/PODIUM – DAY

T.J. slowly gains confidence and comfort.

> **T.J.**
> I recently met an uncle I never knew I
> had.

> **DARLENE (V.O.)**
> So, I'm keeping this album to help me
> remember that *I* did that. Not him.

VIDEO IMAGE OF DARLENE

> **DARLENE**
> And if you don't mind, I'm going to skip
> out early because I've got a date!

Darlene must walk out of frame on the limp applause of
only one or two women.

> **T.J. (V.O.)**
> In a way, keeping that from me was an
> act of violence. Especially since no one
> will tell me why.

EXT. INGERSOLL HOME – NIGHT

Two stories. Front porch. Breezeway. Garage. A picket fence.

A TAXI CAB pulls up.

KEVIN INGERSOLL emerges slowly. He wears a dark suit. No luggage.

The DOOR BELL sounds as he regards the house.

INT. FRONT DOOR — NIGHT

T.J. pulls the door open. Kevin had expected someone else.

> T.J.
> Can I help you?

> BARBARA
> *(off)* Who is it, T.J.?

> KEVIN
> You're Teresa Jane.

> T.J.
> I know who I am. Who are you?

> KEVIN
> Your Uncle Kevin.

Barbara comes up behind T.J., and upon seeing Kevin, goes on alert.

BARBARA
Go and get your grandfather.

T.J.
He says he's my uncle.

BARBARA
Do as I say.

Barbara turns T.J. away from the door.

BARBARA
Go.

INT. STAGE/PODIUM — DAY

T.J. is winning over some of the audience.

T.J.
His wife was killed down in Texas.

AUDIENCE MEMBER
Whoa...awesome!

The auditorium percolates with laughter.

T.J.
It is not awesome.

T.J. is more spontaneous now, more herself.

INT. LIVING ROOM/STAIRS/HALL – NIGHT

T.J. sprawls on the couch. Kevin is oblivious in a chair. Stephen works the floor. Barbara commands the room.

                    KEVIN
She was having lamb.


                   BARBARA
We saw it on CNN. A soldier gone rogue
down in Dallas.


                    KEVIN
Thought she hated lamb.


                   BARBARA
Too many turn-around deployments or
something.


                    KEVIN
I walked away from the grave.


                   STEPHEN
Anyone know where you are?


                   BARBARA
He could use a doctor.


                    KEVIN
No idea where I was headed.


                   BARBARA
Put him in a cab to a hospital.


                    KEVIN
She died instantly.


                   BARBARA
We can't handle this.

KEVIN
I had to identify the body.

STEPHEN
What about your job?

KEVIN
Work for myself.

STEPHEN
Should we call someone?

KEVIN
Airport nearly did me in.

BARBARA
T.J., go up to your room.

T.J.
What did I do?

KEVIN
Got on the first flight out.

STEPHEN
This is your home.

BARBARA
It is not!

KEVIN
Is it safe here?

STEPHEN
You didn't bring anything?

KEVIN
I heard: *Saint Louis* and handed them a
credit card.

STEPHEN
How did you get to Springfield?

KEVIN
Taxi.

STEPHEN
From Saint Louis?

KEVIN
Had to identify her body.

BARBARA
Did you hear me?

T.J.
I want to listen.

BARBARA
This is adult conversation.

STEPHEN
You're perfectly safe here.

BARBARA
He is not staying.

KEVIN
Lamb.

STEPHEN
Your room is now the guest room.

BARBARA
This is my house too.

STEPHEN
We'll figure this out.

BARBARA
I will not be ignored.

STEPHEN
For God's sake.

BARBARA
Don't give me that.

STEPHEN
Where's your compassion?

T.J. takes Kevin by the hand.

BARBARA
Same place his was when you were on
life support in ICU.

STEPHEN
Man's been kicked in the teeth.

BARBARA
I don't care.

Follow as T.J. leads him up the stairs.

                         STEPHEN
          Forgive him.

                         BARBARA
          I've seen you sit in that chair and curse him.

T.J. leads Kevin down the upstairs hallway.

                         STEPHEN
          *(off)* There's nothing else to do.

                         BARBARA
          *(off)* Pathetic.

INT. GUEST ROOM — NIGHT

T.J. leads Kevin in and over to the bed.

                         KEVIN
          Is it safe here?

                         T.J.
          Don't be afraid.

Kevin turns and sits on the bed and looks back at T.J.,
but in her place he sees his ten year old self:

YOUNG KEVIN.

                         KEVIN
          She hated lamb.

                         YOUNG KEVIN
          Where have you been?

                    KEVIN
     I don't know.

                YOUNG KEVIN
     You ditched me.

                    KEVIN
     I don't remember.

INT. GUEST ROOM — DAY

Barbara charges in.

                  BARBARA
     What's going on in here?

                     T.J.
     Nothing.

                  BARBARA
     It's time for bed.

T.J. reluctantly crosses out in front of her.

                  BARBARA
     You had no business coming her this way.

                    KEVIN
     They could have said Beirut, I would have
     handed them my credit card.

Barbara leaves, closing the door behind her.

                YOUNG KEVIN
     Why have you come back?

Kevin turns to see Young Kevin on the bed behind him, hands clasped behind his head on the pillow.

                    KEVIN
          Something pulled me here.

                    YOUNG KEVIN
          You going to stay?

                    KEVIN
          She'd been shot in the head.

EXT. ABRAHAM LINCOLN'S TOMB – NIGHT

Darlene and Harry Millet kiss near the LINCOLN MAUSOLEUM on a small knoll overlooking Springfield Cemetery.

                    HARRY
          Wonder what Abraham would have to say
          about all this romance on his grave?

                    DARLENE
          Kind of spooky, isn't it?

                    HARRY
          I think he'd say: *Don't you people have
          homes to go to?*

                    DARLENE
          The fun of having a secret getting a little
          old?

                    HARRY
I'm going to tell your father. He's been
my friend too long

                   DARLENE
Does this mean I can start spreading it
around that I've got a boyfriend?

                    HARRY
Boyfriend sounds like high-school.

                   DARLENE
T.J. already suspects.

                    HARRY
Never was good at sneaking around.

Harry heads off down the knoll.

                   DARLENE
I kind of like it.

                    HARRY
C'mon, I'll show you my plot.

Darlene runs to take his hand.

                   DARLENE
Okay, then I'll show you mine.

EXT. INGERSOLL HOME/GARAGE — DAY

Stephen works at the bench. The garage door is open.
Harry approaches with a full mailbag.

STEPHEN
Still sleeping in your uniform?

HARRY
How's Kevin?

STEPHEN
What's on your shoe?

Harry studies his shoes.

HARRY
What the heck is that?

STEPHEN
Walter, Ben, Tyrone, how is everyone?

HARRY
Chester wants out on disability.

STEPHEN
He's been angling for that since day one.

HARRY
Picked up one too many hundred-pound
sacks. Says he ruptured something. Still
doing tests at Memorial.

STEPHEN
Let him lie around awhile and try to make
sense of all the time on his hands.

HARRY
Chester's not like me or you.

STEPHEN
Give anything to be working.

HARRY
Joanie's taking up a collection.

Stephen takes a bill from his wallet and gives it to Harry.

STEPHEN
I'll have to get over to see him.

They head inside through the breezeway.

INT. HOUSE/VARIOUS/CONTINUOUS —DAY

BREEZEWAY

Stephen kicks the mat into place on the back stoop.

HARRY
Something I want to tell you.

STEPHEN
Got time for coffee?

HARRY
I'm running late.

STEPHEN
You're always running late.

KITCHEN

Stephen takes a couple of mugs out of a cabinet and
prepares to pour coffee.

HARRY
Someone's back is up today.

STEPHEN
Tired of the same ole bull.

HARRY
That nails it on the head.

STEPHEN
Thought I had sent him out of here
equipped. Evidently not.

HARRY
Fortified him to absorb his wife taking
a bullet, did you?

Stephen bristles on this jab from Harry.

STEPHEN
Follow me.

STAIRCASE

Harry slowly follows up.

HARRY
I don't want to disturb him.

STEPHEN
We're all disturbed at the moment. It's
worth a try.

UPSTAIRS HALLWAY

Stephen raps a knuckle on Kevin's door.

HARRY
I really do need to talk to you.

STEPHEN
Kevin? Harry Millet's here. Going to have
some coffee.

No response.

STEPHEN
Fresh brewed.

No response.

STEPHEN
Know he'd like to see you.

Stephen elbows Harry to say something.

HARRY
Hey, there, Kevin, Harry Millet here. That
coffee's mighty good.

INT. KEVIN'S ROOM — DAY

Stubble darkens Kevin's face as he sits on the floor, his
back against a wall. He stares vacantly at nothing.

Stephen and Harry are heard through the door.

HARRY
(*off*) Bet you can smell it.

Kevin remains still.

> HARRY
> *(off)* Wife got shot up pretty bad down
> there in Dallas, eh? Sorry to hear that—

> STEPHEN
> *(off)* Mother-a-God! Kevin, we'll be in
> the kitchen, you feel like joining us.

They can be heard retreating down the hall.

> STEPHEN
> *(off)*...hell's the matter with you?

> HARRY
> *(far off)* What?

Commotion is heard from inside the closet.

Young Kevin emerges with a pair of high-cut sneakers.

> YOUNG KEVIN
> Remember these?

> KEVIN
> PF Flyers.

> YOUNG KEVIN
> Not bad, huh?

> KEVIN
> No sleep until we got 'em.

YOUNG KEVIN
Sometimes I wear 'em to bed.

KEVIN
You might want to curb that.

YOUNG KEVIN
Why?

KEVIN
Mom.

YOUNG KEVIN
She doesn't like us, does she?

KEVIN
It's complicated.

YOUNG KEVIN
What happens?

KEVIN
You toughen up.

YOUNG KEVIN
When?

KEVIN
Little bit every day.

YOUNG KEVIN
I don't feel tough.

KEVIN
You will.

                    YOUNG KEVIN
     Soon?

                        KEVIN
     Be patient.

                    YOUNG KEVIN
     Are we happy?

                        KEVIN
     No.

                    YOUNG KEVIN
     Why not?

                        KEVIN
     Something happened.

                    YOUNG KEVIN
     What?

                        KEVIN
     She was having lamb.

INT. KITCHEN — DAY

Harry sits at the kitchen table with his soiled shoe in his
hand.

                        HARRY
     Can't figure out what the heck it is.

                        STEPHEN
     Shoes are your back. Your back is your life.

Harry puts the shoe back on.

                    HARRY
          How's Barb holding up?

                    STEPHEN
          Take a guess.

                    HARRY
          Well, thought I should ask anyway.

                    STEPHEN
          Never right between the two of them
          from the get-go.

                    HARRY
          Just trying to be polite.

                    STEPHEN
          I'm going to tell you something.

                    HARRY
          Okay, you first then.

                    STEPHEN
          Kevin is the reason we had to get married
          way back when.

                    HARRY
          Hate to misconstrue that.

                    STEPHEN
          I got to spell it out?

                    HARRY
Might help.


                    STEPHEN
No big deal now, but it was back then.


                    HARRY
So it's what I thought.


                    STEPHEN
I took responsibility.


                    HARRY
We both knew fellas had to leave town.


                    STEPHEN
Not my style.


                    HARRY
Course it wasn't. Not you.


                    STEPHEN
She wanted to take care of it.


                    HARRY
Wondered how you ended up with a
classy lady like Barb.


                    STEPHEN
We went up to Chicago. The Projects.
Back alley stuff. Filthy.


                    HARRY
That information will never leave this
room.

STEPHEN
He knows. Simple arithmetic.

HARRY
Heck of a thing.

STEPHEN
She resented him.

HARRY
Not sure I want to hear anymore.

STEPHEN
Came home one night, must have been
midnight. The good days. All the overtime
you wanted. February.

HARRY
That coffee ready?

Stephen pours the coffee then opens the back door,
tormented with memory.

STEPHEN
He was sitting on the stoop.

HARRY
Before you built the breezeway.

STEPHEN
She had locked him out.

HARRY
Coffee's good.

STEPHEN
Didn't even want to ask.

HARRY
Be child abuse today.

STEPHEN
Just unlocked the door and left it open
behind me.

HARRY
Seed to your coronary could have been
planted right there.

STEPHEN
I am not proud of it.

HARRY
Always thought you were a good father.

STEPHEN
Had myself fooled.

HARRY
Even tempered. Decent provider.

STEPHEN
Thought work was enough.

HARRY
There's one thing for sure.

STEPHEN
What?

HARRY
No one ever suspected that Barb put out.

Stephen levels an eviscerating cut of the eyes on Harry
and waits for him to feel it.

HARRY
What...?

EXT. OLD ILLINOIS STATE CAPITOL — DAY

School buses line the perimeter.

TOUR GUIDE (V.O)
The building served as the Illinois State
Capitol until 1876.

INT. LEGISLATIVE GALLERY — DAY

School children are massed along the railing listening to
the Tour Guide down in the old House Chamber.

TOUR GUIDE
This chamber was the scene of many
important debates.

The Donahue Twins lean perilously over the railing

TOUR GUIDE
Stephen Douglas served as a Legislator
here. And Ulysses S. Grant was a
familiar face.

Barbara snatches the twins to safety.

TOUR GUIDE
President Lincoln was laid in State here
after his assassination.

INT. CAPITOL STAIRCASE — DAY

T.J. maneuvers next to Barbara who monitors children
descending the stairs.

T.J.
How come I never knew about Uncle Kevin?

BARBARA
We'll discuss that at home.

T.J.
You know we won't.

Barbara turns to herd several stragglers.

INT.  BATHROOM — NIGHT

T.J. is in pajamas. She brushes her teeth. Someone tries
to open the locked door.

T.J.

Ocupado.

T.J. finishes brushing and wipes her mouth.

INT. UPSTAIRS HALLWAY — NIGHT

T.J. comes out and is drawn toward the staircase.

                    T.J. (V.O.)
        It's no secret why I am giving this speech today.

INT. KITCHEN — NIGHT

Kevin draws a glass of water and is drawn toward the
back door.

T.J. observes from the doorway.

                    T.J. (V.O.)
           I have been labeled a bully. It's part of
           my record now.

EXT. BACK STOOP — NIGHT

Young Kevin comes out the back door and sits on the
stoop.

                    T.J. (V.O.)
           I don't feel like a bully.

T.J. takes a seat next to him.

                    T.J. (V.O.)
           I don't think of myself as a bully. Maybe
           that's the problem.

EXT. SCHOOL YARD — DAY

T.J. has a bloody lip. She straddles the chest of WESLEY
BENNETT and is throwing punches.

                    T.J.
        Take it back!

                    WESLEY
          You're a booger-eating dyke!


                     T.J.
          Take it back!


                    WESLEY
          Bet you stand up to take a leak.

A circle of students egg on the fight before an adult pulls
T.J. off of Wesley.


                   T.J. (V.O.)
          In a recent Time Magazine article about
          violence and family, it said...

T.J. is marched into the school building.


                   T.J. (V.O.)
          ...where once family values were thought
          to be protection against violence...

INT. SCHOOL CORRIDOR — DAY

T.J. is wrangled past the opened door of Barbara's
classroom—she comes to the door.


                   T.J. (V.O.)
          ...increasingly they are seen to be the
          cause.

Barbara would like to intercede but does not. She goes
back into her classroom.

INT. HALL OUTSIDE SCHOOL OFFICE – DAY

The school office is enclosed in glass. T.J. goes through the door and heads for the hot seat outside the Principal's Office.

> T.J. (V.O.)
> The article was about a man who blew
> up his family and himself because they
> were about to split apart.

INT. SCHOOL OFFICE — DAY

T.J. smears the blood off her mouth as the Principal's Office door opens and she vaults defiantly inside. The door closes behind her.

> T.J. (V.O)
> He had rigged a bomb to their old station
> wagon.

EXT. STATION WAGON/SILENT — DAY

An old land ark crawls up a steep grade toward the top of a hill.

> T.J. (V.O.)
> The station wagon itself is an emblem of
> traditional family values. You can imagine
> the result.

As the STATION WAGON crests the hill it blows up.

There are no witnesses.

EXT. MAIL ROUTE/CONTINUOUS — DAY

Stephen tags along on Harry's route. He has the fliers and inserts.

> HARRY
> We have this argument everyday.

> STEPHEN
> One of these days you'll give in.

> HARRY
> I'm already courting a Federal offense.

> STEPHEN
> That your final word?

> HARRY
> I want to keep my job.

> STEPHEN
> That's right, Lord it over me.

They arrive at the next mailbox. Stephen opens it, stuffs the junk mail in and holds it open for Harry and the real mail.

> HARRY
> The situation were reversed, would I even
> get the junk?

> STEPHEN
> No.

Harry walks away.

HARRY
You're retired. Go home. Make friends
with your television set.

STEPHEN
What did you want to tell me?

HARRY
I'm not your clown.

STEPHEN
I'm listening. What?

HARRY
You're too busy laughing to listen.

STEPHEN
So, you go to the Lincoln Memorial to talk.
Sounds nice.

HARRY
I am becoming quite a conversationalist.

STEPHEN
So, what's the problem?

At the next house, Stephen sees FRED, another retiree,
unloading groceries from his car. He dashes up to help
him.

FRED
How's the boy?

STEPHEN
No change.

INT. FRED'S KITCHEN — DAY

Fred has to sit down after the exertion. Stephen sets his sacks on the counter.

> STEPHEN
>
> All right?

Fred palms his chest...angina.

> FRED
>
> Got a sister, lost a grandchild out there in San Diego, that shooting at the fast food place.

> STEPHEN
>
> Everyone knows someone.

> FRED
>
> Never got over it.

> STEPHEN
>
> Coronaries or strokes got the rest of us.

> FRED
>
> How's the blood pressure?

> STEPHEN
>
> Good.

> FRED
>
> Cholesterol?

> STEPHEN
>
> Under control.

Fred takes a pill. Stephen draws him a glass of water.

                    FRED
          Mine stinks.

INT. KEVIN'S ROOM — DAY

Young Kevin sits on the bed with his foot on Kevin's
thigh who kneels in front of him and ties the PF Flyers.

                    KEVIN
          A knot at each eye-hole and the laces
          will always stay even.

                    YOUNG KEVIN
          Do the other one too.

Young Kevin switches feet.

                    KEVIN
          Remember they're just shoes.

                    YOUNG KEVIN
          What happens?

                    KEVIN
          Nothing lasts forever.

Young Kevin grabs Kevin by the shirt-front.

                    YOUNG KEVIN
          Tell me!

A FEMALE HAND finds Kevin's shoulder. He turns to see
his wife

MEGAN in a sun dress. The breath rushes out of him.

Young Kevin watches as Kevin embraces her around the waist.

                    KEVIN
          Meg. Oh, Meg.

                    MEGAN
          Shhh...

INT. SCHOOL CORRIDOR — DAY

Barbara marches the Donahue Twins toward the school office.

                    T.J. (V.O.)
          Out in Los Angeles, a middle school
          student was shot by a classmate over a
          Lakers' jacket.

A GUN SHOT is heard.

EXT. UTILITY ALLEY/LOS ANGELES — DAY

A young boy is dead on the ground and is jerked about as the jacket he is wearing is stolen from his corpse.

                    T.J. (V.O.)
          But that's California, right?

INT. OUTSIDE SCHOOL OFFICE – DAY

Barbara holds the glass door as she waits for the Donahue Twins to catch up.

                    T.J. (V.O.)
        Up in Chicago a boy my age was stabbed
        for not giving up his new shoes.


EXT. CHICAGO/SIDEWALK – DAY


A boy lies dead in a pool of blood. His shoes are gone.
One sock has been pulled half off.


                    T.J (V.O)
        That's right here in Illinois.


INT. SCHOOL OFFICE - DAY.


Barbara ushers the Twins inside the office and places a
switch blade on the counter.

                    BARBARA
        She in?

                    CLERK
        She's with someone, actually.

Barbara cuts her eyes toward the Twins.

                    BARBARA
        You know the drill.


The Twins sit on the bench outside the Principal's Office.
Their faces reveal nothing.

                    T.J. (V.O.)
        Violence is the number one killer of kids
        our age no matter where you live.

T.J. emerges from the Principal's Office with a black eye blossoming and a swollen lip.

> BARBARA
> And there's a real shiner.

> PRINCIPAL
> T.J. will be giving a speech about violence
> at our next school assembly.

> T.J.
> Wesley Bennett spit on my new shoes
> and called me a dyke.

> BARBARA
> How's Wesley look?

> PRINCIPAL
> He is at the Emergency Room with a
> broken nose.

Barbara gestures toward the Twins.

> BARBARA
> Concealed weapon. It's on the counter.

The Principal ushers the Twins into her office. Barbara and T.J. head out of the office and down the corridor.

> BARBARA
> See the nurse about that eye. Dyke, huh?

> T.J.
> A booger-eating-dyke.

BARBARA
Well, there goes lunch.

INT. RESTAURANT/LUNCH TIME – DAY

Darlene and several women from her women's group eat lunch in a large booth.

T.J. (V.O.)
Statistically, it is likely I won't live to graduate from high school.

DARLENE
The best thing for an older dog is a younger dog, right?

MARGARET
That would make you a bitch.

CONNIE
What's his name?

DARLENE
I'm not at liberty to say yet.

REBECCA
She's making it up.

DARLENE
Swear!

MARGET
He go commando or are we talking Victor-Viagra here?

Darlene takes too long to answer.

                        REBECCA
            My God, she doesn't know!

                        CONNIE
            And you think I'm desperate.

                        MARGARET
            We know you're desperate.

                        CONNIE
            They haven't slept together yet. So what?

                        DARLENE
            I don't care about that.

                        MARGARET
            This just keeps getting better.

                        REBECCA
            Darlene, honey, no, no, no—

                        CONNIE
            I think it's kind of sweet.

As one, they turn on Connie with derision.

INT. AUDITORIUM STAGE — DAY

T.J. comes to the edge of the stage.

                        T.J.
            Look at the person next to you. Chances
            are one of you won't either.

POV

Students in the audience look at each other in a new light—a sobering moment.

EXT. MAIL ROUTE – DAY

Stephen and Harry head to the next house.

> HARRY
> The problem is her family.

> STEPHEN
> This woman an adult?

> HARRY
> Very much so.

> STEPHEN
> What business is it of the family's?

> HARRY
> There's an age difference.

> STEPHEN
> She have children?

> HARRY
> Yes.

> STEPHEN
> A grown-up woman. A parent. Whose company you enjoy. Sue me, I don't see the problem.

HARRY
Well, her parents, actually.

STEPHEN
Things okay in the bedroom?

HARRY
Wouldn't be much of a gentleman if I
answered that, now would I?

STEPHEN
You haven't slept with her yet.

HARRY
No.

STEPHEN
You need to find out of you can handle
this.

HARRY
I don't think we should get into that.

STEPHEN
She could be a nymphomaniac.

HARRY
See, we've gone too far now.

STEPHEN
She could kill you.

At the next mailbox, the homeowner sticks his head out
the door and calls to them.

HOMEOWNER
How's your son?

STEPHEN
No change.

HOMEOWNER
What the hell?

STEPHEN
Breakin' my heart.

HOMEOWNER
They don't make 'em like us anymore.

STEPHEN
Semper Fi.

They are on to the next house.

STEPHEN
You want some Viagra?

HARRY
Let's not go there.

Stephen faces off with Harry.

STEPHEN
How long's it been?

HARRY
I'd rather not say.

STEPHEN
You don't remember.

HARRY
End of discussion.

STEPHEN
Nothing to be ashamed of.

HARRY
I'm not ashamed.

They continue on to the next house.

STEPHEN
Just don't put pressure on yourself.

HARRY
We need to change the subject. Now.

STEPHEN
The brain is the biggest sexual organ
we've got. Trick is not to over-think it.

HARRY
Never occurs to me to think.

STEPHEN
Just saying, you need the little blue pill,
I gotcha covered.

HARRY
Good God, make him stop.

                              STEPHEN
                    No one needs to know.

                              HARRY
                    Going to boomerang like a heat-seeking
                    missile.

Harry tries to put distance between them.

                            T.J. (V.O)
                    Let me throw out some place-names.
                    Mose Lake, Bethel, Paducah, Stamps.

INT. KEVIN'S ROOM – DAY

It is now Young Kevin who embraces Meg around the
waist.

                               MEG
                    I always knew this about you.

                              KEVIN
                    What?

Meg rakes the boy's hair with her fingers.

                               MEG
                    This.

Meg disengages, removes her shoes, and heads for the
door.

                              KEVIN
                    Stay.

                    MEG
It doesn't work that way.

                    KEVIN
Please.

                    MEG
Ask your question.

                    KEVIN
You were with him.

                    MEG
He was with me.

                    KEVIN
You were reaching out.

                    MEG
I wanted to live.

                    KEVIN
You hated lamb.

                    MEG
I'm out of time.

                    KEVIN
Did you love him?

                    MEG
That the child asking, or the man?

                    KEVIN
Did you love me?

Meg moves into his embrace.

                    MEG
          More than you know.

                    KEVIN
          How did I lose you?

                    MEG
          You never lost me.

                    KEVIN
          What happened?

                    MEG
          You never let me in.

                    KEVIN
          Oh, please, do not let that be true.

Meg shakes her head. Kevin's heart is breaking.

                    MEG
          The beach is mine for awhile. Let me
          have it.

Meg opens the door onto sandy beach and white-capped
surf. T.J., in the place of Young Kevin, takes Kevin's
hand. They watch Meg walk gracefully out to the water.

                    T.J. (V.O.)
          Jonesboro, Edinboro, Fayetteville,
          Richmond, Littleton, Conyers.

INT. CLASSROOM — DAY

Barbara is alone in her classroom, seated at her desk, resisting going home.

> T.J. (V.O.)
> Deming, Fort Gibson, Mount Morris,
> Savannah, Lake Worth.

With nothing left to do, she gathers her things, turns off the lights, and leaves.

INT. STAIRCASE LANDING — DAY

T.J. stands on the landing practicing her speech using 3x5 cards.

Kevin sits in a chair placed in front of her for this exercise, to coach her.

> T.J.
> New Orleans, Williamsport,

T.J. drops her cue cards and panics.

> KEVIN
> Take a breath. Pick up the cards.

> T.J.
> What if this happens during the speech?

> KEVIN
> You know this backwards and forwards.
> Trust yourself.

T.J. takes a moment and then continues without the cards.

                    T.J.
          Santee, Granite Hills, Gary.

Kevin offers a thumbs-up.

EXT. MAIL ROUTE – DAY

Stephen has been stopped dead in his tracks.

                    HARRY
          I know it's a big surprise.

                    STEPHEN
          Stick around for the angina.

                    HARRY
          Going to be all right?

                    STEPHEN
          This is odd, Harry. Very odd. You have
          created an odd situation.

                    HARRY
          It's been murder keeping this from you.

                    STEPHEN
          Are you asking permission?

                    HARRY
          I don't like being a sneak.

STEPHEN
Darlene is very fragile.

HARRY
Seems mighty strong to me.

STEPHEN
I would not want her to get hurt again.

HARRY
Farthest thing from my mind.

STEPHEN
And forget about that Viagra business.

HARRY
Tried to head you off there.

STEPHEN
Now how am I going to get *that* out of
my mind?

HARRY
Don't over-think it.

STEPHEN
You haven't got a chance, pal.

HARRY
Barb?

STEPHEN
There's no way.

                    HARRY
Figured you could help there.

                   STEPHEN
I look suicidal to you?

                    HARRY
What was that earlier about getting
involved more?

                   STEPHEN
You had some dental work done, you ran
into Darlene, it had to be a secret?

                    HARRY
I didn't run into her—we got involved.

Stephen hands back the junk mail.

                   STEPHEN
Oddness, Harry. Oddness.

Stephen walks off. Harry watches him go.

INT – BEDROOM/ BATH – NIGHT

Stephen  brushes his teeth while listening to Barbara
who turns down the bed.

                   BARBARA
I remember a black eye or two. I don't
remember meting any out.

                   STEPHEN
Wesley Bennett a tough kid?

BARBARA
Nobody else would stand up to him.

STEPHEN
And she's branded the bully?

BARBARA
She threw the first punch.

Stephen and Barbara get into bed.

STEPHEN
Doesn't seem right.

BARBARA
Zero tolerance for violent behavior at
school.

STEPHEN
She know what a dyke is?

BARBARA
A booger-eating dyke.

STEPHEN
Tough little girl.

BARBARA
She's had to be. Look at her mother.

STEPHEN
How tough are you?

BARBARA
More bark than bite.

STEPHEN
Darlene is seeing Harry. Romantically.

Barbara nearly vaults out of bed.

BARBARA
Get out!

STEPHEN
And it's serious.

BARBARA
He's too old for her.

STEPHEN
He's younger than you think and she's
older than you like to admit.

BARBARA
He's odd.

STEPHEN
Little bit.

BARBARA
You can't be pleased about this.

STEPHEN
I've had time to digest it.

BARBARA
I knew she was sneaking around with
someone.

HARRY
Glad Harry told me and didn't leave it for
Darlene to do.

BARBARA
Here we go again.

Barbara grabs her robe.

STEPHEN
Where are you going?

BARBARA
You expect me to sleep after dropping
that bomb?

STEPHEN
Harry is a good man.

Barbara is at the door.

BARBARA
Good for what?

STEPHEN
He's kind.

BARBARA
So was Richard until he wanted out.

Barbara sweeps out. Her parting shot weighs on
Stephen.

INT. HOSPITAL CORRIDOR — DAY

Stephen carries a foil parcel and looks at room numbers.

                    T.J. (V.O.)
          Tucson, Red Lake, Cold Spring.

INT. HOSPITAL ROOM – DAY

CHESTER watches a television game show.

                    T.J. (V.O.)
          Jacksboro, Essex, Bailey.

                    CHESTER
          Postmaster General, get in here. Thought
          that massive heart attack killed you.

                    STEPHEN
          It did for a minute. Turns out I wasn't
          done yet.

Chester unwraps the parcel.

                    CHESTER
          Wish it was a long-neck.

                    STEPHEN
          My granddaughter made it.

                    CHESTER
          What the hell is it?

                    STEPHEN
          Chocolate steak. Peanut butter gravy.

Chester takes a bite.

                        CHESTER
          Not bad.


                        STEPHEN
          How's the back?


                        CHESTER
          Good for disability, I hope.


                        STEPHEN
          It's all in the shoes, Chester. Few people
          make a proper investment in shoes.


                        CHESTER
          Screw the shoes. I want out.


                        STEPHEN
          I'd go back in a heartbeat if they'd have
          me.


                        CHESTER
          They deny me this, Springfield and all
          of Illinois will understand the meaning of
          *Going Postal.*


                        STEPHEN
          No one likes to work anymore.


                        CHESTER
          You're the only one I know ever loved it.
          Never could figure out who the hell you
          were trying to impress. Government job.

                    STEPHEN
You can tell a lot about a man by the
way he looks at work.

Not much else to say; silence settles in.

                    CHESTER
Want to watch a game?

                    STEPHEN
On my way to the Post Office, actually.
First time back.

                    CHESTER
Tell everyone thanks for the collection.
Meant a lot.

                    STEPHEN
Sure thing.

                    CHESTER
And thanks for the whatever the heck it
was I ate.

                    STEPHEN
You bet.

                    CHESTER
Next time make it a beer.

                    STEPHEN
Take care, Chester.

Chester returns to the television.

EXT. HARRY' HOUSE – DAY

A Prairie Victorian. Lawn. Shrubs. Neat. No flowers.

Harry and Darlene pull into the driveway in Harry's
pickup truck.

> T.J. (V.O.)
> Cazenovia, Dover, Blacksburg, Nickel
> Mines, Cleveland, Baton Rouge.

Darlene surveys the property as they make their way
onto the porch and the front door.

> DARLENE
> We used to ring your doorbell and run.

> HARRY
> Still get a lot of that.

> DARLENE
> Thought the place was haunted.

> HARRY
> Was for awhile.

> DARLENE
> Careful. I have issues.

> HARRY
> You get used to them.

> DARLENE
> I know you're kidding.

                    HARRY
        Maybe. Maybe not.

Darlene swats him in jest.

                    DARLENE
        Not funny, Harry.

                    HARRY
        Come on in. See for yourself.

                    DARLENE
        You are kidding, right?

INT. ENTRY HALL/LIVING ROOM – DAY

Paint-By-Numbers pictures in which horses feature
prominently populate the walls.

                    HARRY
        We were always a queer lot from when
        that word meant peculiar.

                    DARLENE
        Who's the artist?

                    HARRY
        Right behind you.

                    DARLENE
        Ever tried painting without the numbers?

                    HARRY
        Only color I know anything about is gray.

                    DARLENE
          You like horses.

                    HARRY
          Noble creatures.

INT. BEDROOM – DAY

The newest furniture in the house.

                    HARRY
          Hungry? I've got ham for sandwiches.
          There's Campbell's, if you like Pepper Pot.

                    DARLENE
          Your parent's room?

                    HARRY
          Mine now. Always liked the view out
          front. And what with the ghosts in the
          back rooms, I thought, why not?

                    DARLENE
          Knock it off, Mister. Furniture looks new.

                    HARRY
          Bought it after Mother went. Stripped the
          wallpaper; too many clocks. Gave it a
          coat of paint.

                    DARLENE
          Your favorite color.

                    HARRY
          Suits me.

DARLENE
I like it.

HARRY
Nothing fancy.

Darlene turns to him from the window.

DARLENE
Can we skip the lunch part?

HARRY
Fine by me.

DARLENE
I'm kind of nervous.

HARRY
I've imagined this for a very long time.

Darlene moves into Harry's embrace. They kiss tenderly.

INT. BEDROOM/BED — DAY

They are playful, having discovered comfort with each other. Harry laughs eerily like a ghost. Not bad.

DARLENE
You are awful!

HARRY
(ghostly) Who's the babe, Harry?

DARLENE
My brother used to do that. He knew it
bugged me.

HARRY
*(ghostly)* She looks like a keeper.

DARLENE
Men—nothing but torment. Daddy's on
board. Mom is not going to be so easy.

HARRY
I'll have to turn on the ole Millet charm.

DARLENE
She thinks you're odd.

HARRY
 My father used to say: *Edna-Mae, that
boy ain't right.*

DARLENE
What would she say?

HARRY
*Well, he does take after your side.*

DARLENE
They had humor.

HARRY
We'd have been nowhere without it.

DARLENE
Edna-Mae and...?

HARRY
Raymond Henry Millet. Everyone called him Satchel.

DARLENE
You know I'm going to ask.

HARRY
Had no rear-end whatsoever. Joke was, you could pack everything that might be needed for a road trip in the seat of his trousers.

DARLENE
Roll over.

HARRY
What for?

DARLENE
I want to see if you take after him.

HARRY
I am not showing you my backside.

DARLENE
You couldn't take your hands off mine.

HARRY
World of difference.

DARLENE
You're going to have to tell me how.

HARRY
A lady's behind is a thing of beauty. A
man's is just some ole thing to cushion a
chair.

DARLENE
Women like 'em.

HARRY
Pretty fresh, aren't you? A little spankin'
might be in order here.

Darlene curls down onto Harry's shoulder and snuggles
close.

DARLENE
And where did you learn how to make
love like that?

HARRY
You've seen my paintings. Not a thing
wrong with my imagination.

DARLENE
Could we do it again?

Harry kisses Darlene with passion.

EXT. BEACH/DUNE BLUFF — DAY

Meg looks up at Kevin silhouetted on a bluff. She walks
into the water. Her skirt blossoms in the surf.

POV

BLUFF

Kevin watches Meg walk into the water. He yaws forward falling off the dune.

INT. KEVIN'S ROOM – THAT INSTANT

Young Kevin completes the yaw as he tumbles onto the bed. He prepares to do it again.

                    KEVIN
          Jumping on the bed is not allowed.

                  YOUNG KEVIN
          Yeah, but it's fun.

INT. FRONT DOOR/HALLWAY – DAY

T.J. comes in with her backpack and her black eye. She hears a loud thump upstairs.

                    T.J.
          Uncle Kevin?

She vaults up the stairs.

INT. KEVIN'S ROOM – DAY

Kevin lies on the bed with a forearm draped over his eyes. He sits up as T.J. enters.

                    T.J.
          You all right?

Kevin regards her black eye.

                    KEVIN
        Getting there.

                    T.J.
        Thought I heard something.

                    KEVIN
        Someone hit you?

                    T.J.
        I guess.

                    KEVIN
        You don't know?

                    T.J.
        Know how to write a speech?

                    KEVIN
        I used to.

                    T.J.
        Good enough. I've got to give one.

                    KEVIN
        This have anything to do with that shiner?

                    T.J.
        God, you stink. Open a window for crying
        out loud.

T.J. heads toward the door.

                    KEVIN
        Do I?

                     T.J.
     You need a towel and a bar of soap.

Kevin sniffs at himself—T.J. is so right.

INT. SHOWER — DAY

Kevin rinses shampoo out of his hair. The steamy hot
water sooths. He is in no hurry.

INT. BATHROOM SINK/MIRROR — DAY

Kevin's face is lathered with shaving cream. He uses a
razor with care.

                  T.J. (V.O.)
       Memphis, Oxnard, DeKalb, Fort
       Lauderdale, Madison.

INT. SCHOOL AUDITORIUM/STAGE — DAY

T.J. has become a polished speaker.

                     T.J.
       Huntsville, Columbus, Walpole. Relax,
       there are more.

INT. BATHROOM – DAY

A towel about his waist, Kevin takes a whiff of his
clothes and realizes they won't do.

                    T.J. (V.O.)
        Chardon, Jacksonville, Aurora, Oakland,
        Springfield...Oregon.

INT. KEVIN'S ROOM – DAY

Kevin opens the closet door and finds a rack of dry-
cleaned Postal Uniforms hanging in plastic garment
bags.

He takes one out and considers it. Not his size, but, hey,
in a pinch.

                    T.J. (V.O.)
        Can you guess what all these towns have
        in common aside from being places in the
        U.S.?

EXT. POST OFFICE/PARKING LOT — DAY

Stephen gets out of his Mustang and slowly climbs the
stairs to the loading dock.

                    T.J. (V.O.)
        Portland, Oak Creek, and last but not
        least...Newtown.

INT. POST OFFICE – DAY

Honeycomb-like workstations (*cases*), canvas carts filled
with parcels, and a labyrinth of conveyor tracks.

                    T.J. (V.O)
        All sights of mass shootings, mostly at
        schools.

Former co-workers offer a warm reception.

                    AD LIBS
        Steve-O!
        Everyone look sharp!
        There he is!
        The General!
        Legendary, Ingersoll!

He shakes hands as people gather.

                    STEPHEN
        Nice to be remembered.

                    WORKER
        Like we could forget you!

                    STEPHEN
        I'm looking for Harry.

                    ANOTHER WORKER
        So is Harry.

Laughter all around. Harry approaches.

                    HARRY
        Sounds like at laugh at someone's
        expense.

                    STEPHEN
        Good to see you all.

The gathering breaks up.

HARRY
Hate to think it was mine.

STEPHEN
Got hand in the cookie jar written all over
you?

HARRY
There a problem with the way I look?

STEPHEN
The condition of that uniform.

HARRY
Only worn it once.

STEPHEN
Do you roll it in a ball at night?

HARRY
I take a ribbing from this crew everyday.
I know you didn't come here just to add
your two cents.

STEPHEN
What's your day off this week?

HARRY
Thursday.

STEPHEN
All right, then, Thursday, be at the house,
seven o'clock sharp. We'll have dinner.
You like lamb?

HARRY
What about Barb?

STEPHEN
I hope you know what you are getting
into here.

HARRY
I'm stable. I own property.

STEPHEN
If you're going to bail. Do it now.

HARRY
Furthest thing from my mind.

STEPHEN
I'm going to bank on that.

HARRY
You won't be disappointed

STEPHEN
I hope not.

HARRY
I'm just starting to live.

STEPHEN
I can tell.

HARRY
Gave up thinking this could ever happen
for me.

STEPHEN
As long as Darlene is happy.

HARRY
What changed your mind?

STEPHEN
I meant it when I said it was time to get
involved.

HARRY
Good man, Stephen.

STEPHEN
Getting there. Seven sharp. And bring
something for Barbara.

HARRY
Like what?

STEPHEN
Flowers.

HARRY
Will do.

Stephen surveys the industry around him.

STEPHEN
I used to own this place.

HARRY
No question about that.

Stephen waves to others as he goes out.

INT. INGERSOLL DEN – DAY

T.J. sits on the floor using the coffee table as a desk. The television is on. She is doing homework. Kevin comes in wearing the uniform.

> T.J.
> And he's gone Postal.

> KEVIN
> I was kind of low-tide there.

> T.J.
> No one touches Grandpa's uniforms.

> KEVIN
> Think he'll mind?

> T.J.
> Too late now.

> KEVIN
> I'm going to have to get to a store to pick up a few things.

> T.J.
> You must be hungry.

> KEVIN
> I am, actually.

EXT. A RAILROAD CAR DINER — DAY

> KEVIN (V.O.)
> This going to ruin your dinner?

INT. DINER/BOOTH – DAY

Wall-mounted Juke Boxes at every booth. Lots of
chrome. Hamburger for T.J.; a sandwich for Kevin.

                    T.J.
        This is dinner.


                    KEVIN
        Your mother and I used to come here
        after school.


                    T.J.
        Together?


                    KEVIN
        She with her friends. Me with mine.


                    T.J.
        Because that would have been weird.


                    KEVIN
        It was the place to hang out.


                    T.J.
        Everyone goes to the mall now.


                    KEVIN
        This was walking-distance.


                    T.J.
        How come I never knew about you until
        you showed up at the door?

KEVIN
Not sure I can answer that.

T.J.
Which means you're not going to.

KEVIN
More like...I don't know.

T.J.
Don't you like us?

KEVIN
Yes.

T.J.
Did something happen?

KEVIN
My life was down in Texas.

T.J.
With your wife.

KEVIN
Megan.

T.J.
Who I'll never meet.

KEVIN
No.

T.J.
What was she like?

KEVIN
Intelligent. Independent.

T.J.
Have a picture?

Kevin takes out his wallet and a picture.

KEVIN
That's a couple of years old.

T.J.
She was beautiful.

KEVIN
Smart. Funny. We laughed a lot. She
was strong.

T.J.
Did you like her?

KEVIN
Of course.

T.J.
I mean, I know you loved her, but did
you like her besides?

KEVIN
I did. Very much.

T.J.
My father has a new family.

KEVIN
That's got to be hard.

T.J.
Wish I could forget about him the way
everyone seemed to have forgotten
about you.

KEVIN
You might not always feel that way.

T.J.
He stopped liking us.

KEVIN
Divorce can be complicated.

T.J.
It's an act of violence.

KEVIN
Okay.

T.J.
I don't have a lot of friends.

KEVIN
Why not?

T.J.
We had to move.

KEVIN
That'll do it.

                    T.J.
Mom maxed out her credit cards and had
to sell the house.

                    KEVIN
Ouch.

                    T.J.
Another act of violence.

                    KEVIN
People move all the time.

                    T.J.
They never liked each other.

                    KEVIN
I'll bet they did at one time.

                    T.J.
I heard him say: *I never actually liked
you.*

                    KEVIN
People say things they may not mean.

                    T.J.
More violence. It's on my mind now.

                    KEVIN
Okay.

                    T.J.
It's in everything. People get used to it.

Kevin considers this.

INT. AUDITORIUM STAGE — DAY

The audience is now rapt.

                    T.J.
          Oh, and Dallas, Texas, home of the Book
          Depository, the grassy knoll, and that...
          *other* Presidential assassination. Here we
          are living in the Land of Lincoln. My uncle
          said I should be sure to include that.

EXT. INGERSOLL HOME — NIGHT

Lights on in the den, while the rest of the house is dark.
Canned television laughter is heard—a ubiquitous
situation comedy.

INT. INGERSOLL DEN — NIGHT

Stephen polishes his shoes. Barbara reads a newspaper.
Darlene lies on the floor and is a headrest for T.J. Kevin
grows restless and leaves the room.

                    T.J. (V.O.)
          He showed me a picture of his wife, my
          aunt, who I'll never get to meet. She was
          beautiful...before she took a bullet hat
          left her nearly impossible to identify.

All eyes follow him out and then connect with each other
asking what it might mean.

EXT. INGERSOLL BACK STOOP — NIGHT

Young Kevin comes out the kitchen door and sits on the stoop. Kevin takes a seat next to him.

More canned television laughter is heard, along with a run of the show's theme music up to a commercial.

EXT. DARLENE'S CAR/MOVING — DAY

Darlene is behind the wheel. Kevin sits shotgun. They pull into the mall parking lot.

> DARLENE
> We had not heard from you in so long
> that by the time she arrived you had
> ceased to be part of the conversation.

> KEVIN
> Ah. Got it. Of course.

> DARLENE
> I take it you weren't pining away for us.

> KEVIN
> I had stopped thinking about the family.

> DARLENE
> My initiation to the fact that men leave.

> KEVIN
> Dad never left.

> DARLENE
> He was never there to begin with.

KEVIN
Ever wonder why?

DARLENE
Yeah, but it got me nowhere.

KEVIN
I figured it had to do with how and why
they got married.

DARLENE
And that's another thing that always
bugged me. I had to follow the straight
and narrow to reclaim the family virtue.
Like I didn't know how to count.

KEVIN
Amazing what you get used to after
enough of it.

DARLENE
I guess.

KEVIN
T.J. said that; it's not mine.

They get out of the car and head inside.

DARLENE
If I had known T.J. was going to like
having an uncle so much, I would have
hired one.

KEVIN
She's a great kid, Darlene. Very smart.

DARLENE
I sometimes wonder which one of us is
the parent?

KEVIN
You did good.

DARLENE
She's all but raising herself.

KEVIN
At least you've done no damage.

DARLENE
Too early to tell. I've been a little
pre-occupied with trying to grow up
myself.

KEVIN
I like her.

DARLENE
How long you going to be in here?

KEVIN
Just need a change of clothes. A few
personal items. I'll be quick.

DARLENE
I am going to look at shoes and I'm
feeling like I want something outrageous.
So take your time. I intend to trash my
comfort zone and everybody else's.

They go in different directions.

EXT. HENSON-ROBINSON ZOO — DAY

Harry and T.J. are in the big-cat-section, pausing at the cages.

                              T.J.
          Do you guys touch tongues when you
          kiss?

                              HARRY
          Sounds gross, doesn't it?

                              T.J.
          I think everything between men and
          women is gross.

                              HARRY
          Your mother thought you and I should
          get to know one another.

                              T.J.
          You're so old.

                              HARRY
          How old do you think I am?

                              T.J.
          Eighty? Eighty-five?

                              HARRY
          You'll be all grown up with kids of your
          own before I see that age.

                              T.J.
          Do you like her?

                    HARRY
Interesting question. Believe I do.


                     T.J.
I didn't say love, I said like.


                    HARRY
I'm not deaf yet.


                     T.J.
What should I call you?


                    HARRY
Answer to most anything. Just don't call
me late to supper.

T.J. snorts an unexpected chuckle.

                     T.J.
You have a middle name?


                    HARRY
Gordon.


                     T.J.
Anyone call you that?


                    HARRY
No.


                     T.J.
They do now, Gordon.


                    HARRY
Doesn't sound bad coming from you.

T.J. skips ahead and turns back

> T.J.
> Let's get to the snake house. Their food
> comes live!

Harry follows, tentatively.

INT. CLASSROOM — DAY

Barbara grades papers at her desk. On the board behind
her is written:

> *I will not use violence to get my way.*

The Donahue Twins sit at their desks, writing. The clock
reads 3:30 p.m.

> BARBARA
> Time's up.

The Twins bring their papers forward.

> BARBARA
> I hope you've learned a lesson.

POV

Barbara reads a page of: *Mrs. Ingersoll stinks.*

And the other of: *Mrs. Ingersoll is a ho.*

She looks up and stares down the BARRELS OF TWO
AUTOMATIC HAND GUNS.

She smiles as she sees water leaking from one, but sobers quickly upon seeing that the other looks to be real.

                    TIMOTHY DONAHUE
          I could shoot you right now.


                    BARBARA
          Please...

THOMAS DONAHUE squirts her in the eye. She cringes and brings a hand to her face.

                    TIMOTHY
          Tell and you're dead.

They train their weapons on her as they leave the room. She is left in disbelief and terror.

INT. MEN'S CLOTHING STORE — DAY

A Salesman holds up a very expensive sports coat.

                    SALESMAN
          This jacket would need no alteration.

It is Harry who slips into the jacket. He is surprised by the way he looks.

                    SALESMAN
          Seldom happens. It was made for you.

                    HARRY
          I'll take it.

EXT. INGERSOLL DRIVEWAY — DAY

Barbara pulls into the driveway and gets the dry-cleaning from the back seat. Kevin is on the porch.

                    KEVIN
          Those look familiar.

Barbara wheels around in surprise.

                    KEVIN
          Whoa, thought you saw me.

Barbara closes the door but remains adrift.

                    BARBARA
          I've just had two boys arrested. Children.

EXT. SCHOOL — DAY

The Donahue Twins, with bound wrists, are assisted into the backs of separate cruisers.

                    KEVIN (V.O.)
          And what was their crime?

                    BARBARA (V.O.)
          Ever stared down the barrel of a gun?

                    KEVIN (V.O.)
          No.

Timothy Donahue locks eyes with Barbara as his cruiser pulls out.

EXT. DRIVEWAY — DAY

Kevin has come closer.

                    BARBARA
          You see things.

                    KEVIN
          Try looking into an open grave.

                    BARBARA
          Yes. Of course. I am sorry for your loss.

                    KEVIN
          You would've approved of her, I think.

                    BARBARA
          I doubt it's in me to approve of anything.

                    KEVIN
          She'd have won you over.

                    BARBARA
          So much has dislodged itself since you
          showed up at the door.

                    KEVIN
          No argument from me.

                    BARBARA
          I knew going in I wasn't going to be any
          good at motherhood.

KEVIN
This because of these two boys, or
because I showed up at the door?

BARBARA
I have always hated to fail.

KEVIN
I know.

BARBARA
I felt trapped.

KEVIN
I think I saw that.

BARBARA
I felt like I was in it alone.

KEVIN
Seemed like you ran the show.

BARBARA
Your father did what he could; do not
misunderstand me.

KEVIN
Never having been a parent, I try not to
judge. Heavy on the *try*.

BARBARA
Did I have anything to do with that?

KEVIN
I'll say no.

BARBARA
Your sister seems to feel I was at cause
for everything.

KEVIN
It had to do with me and Megan and
never actually talking about it.

BARBARA
Was it I who kept you away?

KEVIN
Look, I can't say for sure why I showed
up here, but I don't think it had anything
to do with balancing the books.

BARBARA
Did you find happiness?

KEVIN
Not long ago I would have said yes.

BARBARA
You were not an unhappy child.

KEVIN
It was my job to be happy.

BARBARA
I suspect you're right about that.

KEVIN
I have always hated to fail, too.

BARBARA
You were the light in every room. It was
almost unnatural.

KEVIN
Felt like we were all going down and I
was the only one who knew how to swim.

BARBARA
You could not be extinguished.

KEVIN
There came a point.

BARBARA
Yes. I need to tell you something.

KEVIN
Am I going to want to hear this?

BARBARA
I may never be able to say it again.

KEVIN
Those two boys must have done a job on
you.

BARBARA
A pair of sneakers, an insignia at the
ankle.

KEVIN
PF Flyers.

BARBARA
You kept wearing them to bed.

KEVIN
I loved them.

BARBARA
Which is why I burned them.

KEVIN
I wondered.

BARBARA
But, then, you got over that too.

KEVIN
No I didn't.

BARBARA
Bounced right back.

KEVIN
I learned not to want, not to need.

BARBARA
I will take that to my grave.

KEVIN
I'm beginning to get an idea of what
Megan took to hers.

They remain adrift together in the driveway.

BARBARA
What's to become of us?

                    KEVIN
        It already has.

Barbara nods in acknowledgement and walks away.

Kevin watches her go into the house.

INT. BEAUTY PARLOR — DAY

Darlene is nervous as the stylist pulls strands of her hair
through holes in a plastic cap.

                    STYLIST
        Trust me.

                    DARLENE
        I want something edgy.

                    SYLIST
        No problem.

More than courageous, Darlene is determined.

INT. T.J.'s BEDROOM — DAY

T.J. stands at a mirror wearing a dress with her new
athletic shoes.

                    T.J. (V.O.)
        How did you feel about the way we all
        had to enter the building this morning?

The dress won't do.

INT. SCHOOL ENTRANCE — MORNING

Students wait to enter through a metal detector.

INT. METAL DETECTOR ARBOR — DAY

T.J. is waved forward into the gate where she waits for another signal to exit.

> T.J. (V.O.)
> I don't know about you, but I felt like a criminal.

INT. T.J.'s BEDROOM — DAY

T.J. stands in front of the mirror wearing a skirt and blouse and her new athletic shoes.

> T.J. (V.O.)
> I used to love coming to school. But not anymore.

This outfit won't do either.

INT. MEN'S SHOE DEPARTMENT — DAY

Harry is fitted for a new pair of dress shoes.

> T.J. (V.O.)
> Here's what I really want to say.

INT. T.J.'s BEDROOM — DAY

T.J. stands in front of the mirror in jeans and T-shirt and her new athletic shoes.

> T.J. (V.O.)
> I think violence and happiness are very
> much alike. Why?

This outfit is perfect

INT. DARLENE'S BEDROOM — DAY

Darlene studies her edgy new hair style and color in the
mirror. She likes it.

> T.J. (V.O.)
> Because we're never prepared for either
> one.

INT. GARAGE — DAY

Stephen upends the kitchen waste basket into a large
trash can.

> T.J. (V.O.)
> Maybe that should be the subject of
> someone else's speech.

INT. BREEZEWAY/DOOR STOOP — DAY

Stephen pauses at the stoop...that old memory
rekindled.

> T.J. (V.O.)
> What Is Happiness? I have no idea.

INT. KITCHEN — DAY

ON Darlene's outrageous new shoes as she steps aside to let Stephen slide the waste basket in under the sink.

> T.J. (V.O.)
> Is Wesley Bennett here?

FOLLOW Darlene into the dining room.

INT. DINING ROOM — DAY

Darlene tosses a dish towel to Kevin.

> DARLENE
> Hit the glassware, Tex. They look like
> they have leprosy.

Kevin uses the towel to spiff up the wine glasses. Darlene sets the silverware.

> KEVIN
> Does T.J. spend a lot of time with her
> father?

> DARLENE
> Less and less. He's got another one on
> the way.

> KEVIN
> So she said.

> DARLENE
> Double income, no kids. You must have
> done all right.

KEVIN
I don't know. All we did was work. Think
we bought into the wrong bill of goods.

Stephen comes to the doorway.

STEPHEN
Anyone want gravy?

DARLENE
Harry will, I'll bet. He's strictly meat and
potatoes.

STEPHEN
Lamb gravy has got the viscosity of
crankcase oil.

Kevin goes on alert.

KEVIN
Lamb?

DARLENE
Hello.

STEPHEN
Tastes like it, too.

KEVIN
That's what I smell, lamb?

STEPHEN
Saw the recipe on TV. It was not served
with gravy.

                         KEVIN
           I'm not going to...I'm sorry, I can't.

Kevin tosses the towel on the table and flees the room.

                        STEPHEN
           What just happened?

                        DARLENE
           Well, let's think about that. His wife's last
           meal, what was it? Oh, right, lamb.

                        STEPHEN
           *(beat)* Mother of God.

                        DARLENE
           Yeah.

EXT. RESTAURANT — EVENING

A minivan pulls into a parking space. T.J. drops out of
the shotgun seat. Her father,

RICHARD HUNNICUT, middle-management-plump, gets
a stroller out of the back.

PAULA, his enormously pregnant wife, un-straps a one-
year-old,

JEREMY, from the safety seat in the middle.

                        RICHARD
           You couldn't wear a dress to your
           birthday dinner at a restaurant?

                    T.J.
          I hate that sissy-stuff.


                    PAULA
          Sweetheart you could look so pretty in
          pink or yellow.


All head toward the restaurant.


                    RICHARD
          And I can't wait to hear what that black
          eye is about.


                    PAULA
          These babies have taken the wind out of
          me.


INT. BEDROOM — EVENING


Stephen opens the door allowing a shaft of hallway light
to cut across Barbara who lies in the dark on the bed.


                    STEPHEN
          Any better?


                    BARBARA
          Feels like an ice pick has been driven into
          my skull.


                    STEPHEN
          Well, this evening is shaping up to be a
          real winner.


                    BARBARA
          I can get this under control.

STEPHEN
Why didn't someone slap me when I
came home with that leg of lamb?

BARBARA
Talking to the wrong person, chum. I've
been black-balled from my own kitchen
thanks to someone's forced retirement.

STEPHEN
Harry will be here soon.

BARBARA
Anymore I just come when called. Do not
expect me to eat.

STEPHEN
Can I get you anything?

BARBARA
Get rid of that light.

Stephen goes out and closes the door behind him.

INT. RESTAURANT — NIGHT

Jeremy sits in a highchair. Richard gnaws a drumstick.
T.J. picks at her food. Paula is between helpings.

PAULA
God help me, I'm still hungry.

INT. INGERSOLL LIVING ROOM — NIGHT

Harry shows off his new sport coat.

HARRY
Imagine me in silk?

STEPHEN
What's that on your shoe?

Harry looks down.

HARRY
Now what the heck is that?

DARLENE
Very handsome.

HARRY
They're brand new.

Barbara enters...a trouper.

BARBARA
That cannot be Harry Millet.

HARRY
Evening, Barb.

BARBARA
You two have brought out some style in
each other, haven't you?

HARRY
Little sassy maybe. We could both do with
more of that.

DARLENE
A lot more of that.

Stephen hands Harry a dish towel

                    STEPHEN
          Here, wipe that shoe.

Harry does as he is told.

                    HARRY
          Some flowers there for you. On the table.

                    BARBARA
          Well, Harry, you are full of surprises.

INT. RESTAURANT — NIGHT

Paula is uncomfortable. Richard continues eating. T.J. is
through with food.

                    T.J.
          I want to ask you guys something. It's for
          school.

                    RICHARD
          Shoot.

                    T.J.
          Just say the first thing that comes into
          your mind.

                    PAULA
          Hairspray.

All look at Paula.

PAULA
I smell Aqua Net.

T.J.
What does violence mean to you?

RICHARD
The wrong interest rate.

Paula sits up in sudden distress.

RICHARD
You all right?

PAULA
Guess whose water just broke?

Richard throws down a chicken bone and wipes his mouth.

INT. INGERSOLL DINING ROOM — NIGHT

All are seated around the table; dinner has just been served. Wine glasses are refilled.

HARRY
Word is no disability for Chester.

STEPHEN
That right?

HARRY
And he is on the warpath.

                    DARLENE
Nice wine, Harry.


                    HARRY
Told them I needed something fit for a
celebration.


                    BARBARA
New hair. New clothes. My mother's bone
china. Enough celebrating!


                    HARRY
What do you say, Darlene, should we pull
out the stops?


                    DARLENE
Harry.


                    HARRY
I'm about ready to bust.

EXT. INGERSOLL HOME — NIGHT

The minivan pulls up long enough to drop off T.J. Kevin
sits on the front porch steps.


                    KEVIN
Chew with your mouth open or something?


                    T.J.
They're about to have their baby.


                    KEVIN
World is full of relatives.

T.J. joins him on the front stoop.

> ### T.J.
> Ever get so mad you had to break
> something?

> ### KEVIN
> I'll say yes.

> ### T.J.
> What?

> ### KEVIN
> Someone's heart.

> ### T.J.
> Whose?

> ### KEVIN
> Maybe my own.

> ### T.J.
> Why are you out here; shoot your drink
> through you nose or something?

Kevin laughs at the joke back on him. Have we seen that
before...*Kevin actually laughing?*

> ### KEVIN
> Front stoop, back stoop, best seats in the
> house. Always were. Trying to figure out
> how to get myself home.

> ### T.J.
> Wish I could go with you.

                    KEVIN
Not too well fixed for visitors at the
moment.

                     T.J.
I mean for good.

Kevin gets up wanting to move.

                    KEVIN
And I wish I'd taken my wife to see the
ocean.

T.J. joins him as they head down the street.

                     T.J.
How come?

                    KEVIN
She always wanted to see it. And we
were always too busy.

INT. DINING ROOM — NIGHT

Stephen and Barbara have just been broadsided.

                   STEPHEN
You're moving pretty quickly here, aren't
you?

                    HARRY
My intentions became serious as soon as
I knew what they were. They have always
been honorable.

DARLENE
We've got a package deal out in Las
Vegas.

HARRY
Catch a 9 o'clock out of Saint Louis
tomorrow night.

DARLENE
We'll be married on Saturday.

HARRY
Might even try my hand at Black Jack.

DARLENE
Back in time for work on Monday.

BARBARA
What's the rush, or do you have another
surprise for us?

DARLENE
I am not pregnant.

BARBARA
Too bad. You really could've rubbed my
nose in it.

STEPHEN
If this is what you two want, then we're
behind you.

BARBARA
Way behind you.

Harry finally takes note of the food on his plate.

                    HARRY
          Hey, wait a minute, this isn't ham.

                    BARBARA
          I will have some of that wine after all.

                    STEPHEN
          Lamb, Harry. I said *Lamb.*

                    HARRY
          Thought sure you'd said *ham.*

                    BARBARA
          Just pass the Goddamned bottle.

                    HARRY
          Can't tolerate lamb.

                    STEPHEN
          If I live through this life, it'll be a miracle.

INT. JETLINER — NIGHT

Harry and Darlene take their seats and buckle in.

                    HARRY
          No turning back now.

                    DARLENE
          Nervous?

                    HARRY
          First time flying.

> DARLENE
> You're going to love it.

Harry pulls out the airsickness bag from the seatback in front of him

> HARRY
> Hope I won't need this.

EXT. RUNWAY/JETLINER — NIGHT

The Jet roars down the runway and rotates up into the night sky. Landing gear up—the plane turns and climbs out of sight.

INT. JETLINER — NIGHT

Darlene is horrified as she watches Harry retching into the airsickness bag. He comes up for air on a Cheshire grin.

> HARRY
> Just kidding.

Darlene swats him on the arm.

EXT.  LAS VEGAS STRIP — NIGHT

A spectacle of lights beyond imagination.

EXT. BELLAGIO HOTEL — NIGHT

Water fountains put on a dazzling show.

INT. HOTEL LOBBY — NIGHT

As they approach the front desk, Harry is a stepchild suddenly come upon a carnival.

                    DARLENE
          Am I going to have to worry about you?

                    HARRY
          Might have to pinch me.

INT. HOTEL ROOM — NIGHT

Harry tips the porter and closes the door. Darlene is at the window with the city laid out below them.

                    DARLENE
          Come see.

Harry joins her at the window. They take each other's hand.

                    HARRY
          Just be tuning into my fishing show at
          home. Bottle of beer. Some Cheetos.
          Paint a little maybe.

EXT. INGERSOLL HOME — NIGHT

All is dark save for the kitchen light.

INT. INGERSOLL KITCHEN — NIGHT

Barbara, in nightgown and robe, pours warm milk into a glass. After a long, quiet moment...

Stephen comes in through the dining room also in
pajamas and robe.

                    STEPHEN
          There enough for two?

Barbara gets a glass from a cabinet and shares her milk
with him.

                    BARBARA
          You were snoring like a bull dozer when
          I left the room.

                    STEPHEN
          Going to tell me what's wrong?

                    BARBARA
          There's nothing wrong.

                    STEPHEN
          Might help.

                    BARBARA
          I doubt it.

                    STEPHEN
          Might help me.

                    BARBARA
          I was hoping for a little peace and quiet.

                    STEPHEN
          Business as usual won't work anymore.

BARBARA
Excuse me?

STEPHEN
I was content to ride things out. It won't
let me.

BARBARA
Go back to bed.

STEPHEN
Two c-notes, and you have to lie on a
sheet on the floor.

BARBARA
Please. Not tonight.

STEPHEN
Dangerous neighborhood. Derelict
apartment. The filth.

BARBARA
We ever going to be done with this?

STEPHEN
The tools he took out.

BARBARA
*Barbaric—*

STEPHEN
Barbaric. Well, they were!

BARBARA
*You could have died—*

                    STEPHEN
You could have died.

                    BARBARA
Maybe I did.

                    STEPHEN
I had plans, too, you know.

                    BARBARA
I made my bed. But you will not let me
lie in it.

                    STEPHEN
Neither one of us has moved on. We like
to think we have. But we're just fooling
ourselves...everywhere you look.

EXT. BREEZEWAY/STOOP — NIGHT

Kevin sits on the back stoop. Young Kevin is seated next
to him.

                    BARBARA (V.O)
Stop looking. Problem solved.

                    STEPHEN (V.O)
We drove the kids away. Both of them.

Kevin embraces Young Kevin. They can hear everything.

                    BARBARA (V.O)
Life gets tough so they come back? I
didn't get to go back!

                    STEPHEN (V.O)
        I would just like to know why you locked
        him out that time?

                    BARBARA (V.O)
        What are you talking about?

INT. KITCHEN — NIGHT

                    STEPHEN
        I came home the middle of the night.
        He's locked out, freezing cold, on the
        back stoop. He looked so hurt.

                    BARBARA
        Who?

                    STEPHEN
        Kevin. Kevin! My son. Our son.

Kevin comes in the back door, bringing the room to a
halt.

                    KEVIN
        Getting kind of loud out there.

                    BARBARA
        I'm going to bed.

                    KEVIN
        I locked the door.

                    STEPHEN
        What?

KEVIN
I didn't want Mom to know I had snuck
out.

STEPHEN
You locked yourself out?

KEVIN
I was waiting for you.

STEPHEN
Why would you do that?

KEVIN
I wanted you to know that someone was
waiting for you here, and that it was me.

BARBARA
I did my share of waiting.

STEPHEN
*(to Barbara)* I thought it was you.

BARBARA
Evidently. But I have never locked
anybody out of this house.

KEVIN
You stepped over me without a word,
opened the door, and went inside.

BARBARA
That's enough now.

STEPHEN
The way you looked up at me. It was too
much.

KEVIN
Something happened at that moment.
Things changed.

Stephen has been rendered speechless. Barbara takes
him by the hand.

BARBARA
Let's not make a big deal out of who
locked a door so long ago.

KEVIN
It all felt different after that.

The back door opens again and T.J. enters.

BARBARA
Where have you been?

T.J.
Sitting on the stoop with Uncle Kevin.

BARBARA
You should be asleep, Young Lady.

T.J.
Wasn't sleepy.

BARBARA
Go on, now, up to bed.

T.J. reluctantly heads off to her room.

                    KEVIN
    I think it's time for me to book a flight.


                   BARBARA
    Children everywhere I turn. Children.
    Get the light, would you?

Barbara leads Stephen by the hand out through the
dining room.

Kevin pours out their milk and takes his time rinsing the
glasses. He turns out the light.

INT. WEDDING CHAPEL SHOP — MORNING

Harry spins a postcard carousel without much interest.
Is he terrified?

Darlene watches a couple exchange vows before a
Justice of the Peace in the Chapel.

                   JUSTICE
    By the power vested in me by the great
    state of Nevada, I pronounce you man
    and wife.

The couple kiss and pose for a photo.

We HEAR THE OUTSIDE DOOR CHIME.

Darlene turns to see the door closing into place.

Harry has run out on her.

INT. JETLINER/IN FLIGHT — DAY

Darlene has grown deaf to the boozy woman in the aisle
seat next to her.

                        WOMAN
            I've been married five times. Wretched
            men. Both of them.

EXT. INGERSOLL HOME/DRIVEWAY — DAY

Stephen, Barbara, Kevin, and T.J. are just getting into
the family car when a Saint Louis Taxicab pulls up in
front.

Darlene gets out of the cab and makes the long march
over to her family as it slowly dawns on them what must
have happened.

                        DARLENE
            I need three hundred dollars.

                        STEPHEN
            Where's Harry?

                        DARLENE
            He won't give me my luggage until I pay.

Barbara takes several bills out of her purse. Stephen
dips into his wallet. T.J. offers a handful of change.
Kevin heads for the cab.

                        KEVIN
            I'll handle this.

STEPHEN
What happened?

DARLENE
I think that's obvious, isn't it?

STEPHEN
That son-of-a-pup.

DARLENE
Go ahead, say it: *I told you so; fool;
desperate; weak; pathetic...*

BARBARA
Even at my worst, I was never as cruel
to you as you are to yourself.

DARLENE
I had just decided to be happy. God
knows I had tried everything else.

Darlene retreats into the house with her tail between her
legs.

BARBARA
Were I any kind of parent, I'd be right on
her heels with a word of comfort.

STEPHEN
He has crossed the wrong man.

BARBARA
Here I stand.

Kevin returns with Darlene's suitcase and sets it down.

KEVIN
I'm going to take the cab back to Saint
Louis. Save you the drive.

STEPHEN
I like to drive.

KEVIN
Darlene okay?

BARBARA
She'll get through it.

T.J.
I wanted to see you off at the airport.

KEVIN
Have to say goodbye here.

T.J. dives at Kevin and wraps her arms around him.

T.J.
I don't want you to go!

KEVIN
Never occurred to me that I was going
to make a friend here.

T.J.
Can I come visit?

KEVIN
Let's hold onto that idea.

T.J.
If I write, will you write back?

KEVIN
Yes.

T.J.
I can't say goodbye. I just can't

T.J. runs into the house to hide her tears.

STEPHEN
So many things to say.

KEVIN
I needed somewhere to go a little
crazy for awhile.

STEPHEN
My father always told me: *You don't
wonder if I love you; you'll see it in
the way I get up and go to work every
day.*

KEVIN
You used to say that too.

STEPHEN
I did what I knew to do.

KEVIN
I don't doubt that.

STEPHEN
Here we are at goodbye again.

KEVIN
Feels different this time.


STEPHEN
I wish now I'd done more.


KEVIN
I'm struggling with that too.


Stephen thrusts out his hand. They shake.


STEPHEN
Safe travel.


Stephen snags the suitcase and goes inside.


BARBARA
There he goes picking up my slack again.
He always chose me. I made sure of that.


KEVIN
Feels like I was summoned here by
something...what?


Barbara embraces Kevin.


BARBARA
We've all got things calling us back, Kevin.

INT. CAB/BACK SEAT/MOVING — DAY

As the cab pulls away, Young Kevin kneels up on the
seat next to Kevin, to look back at the house.

                    YOUNG KEVIN
          Will we ever see them again?

                       KEVIN
          I don't know.

POV

FRONT SEAT

The driver looks up into the rearview mirror at Kevin
alone in the back.

                      DRIVER
          You say something?

                       KEVIN
          I'm in no hurry.

INT. SCHOOL AUDITORIUM/STAGE — DAY

T.J. scans the audience.

                        T.J.
          Wesley, are you here?

Wesley Bennett stands up.

                      WESLEY
          Here I am.

Silence fills the auditorium. Wesley has put himself at
risk in becoming so conspicuous.

                  T.J.
Wesley, everyday I get up mad. I come
to school mad. I go home mad.

               WESLEY
Me too.

Agreement percolates throughout the audience.

                  T.J.
I can't remember when it wasn't like that.

               WESLEY
I like you, T.J. I never knew how to tell
you.

The auditorium swells with laughter and snickering.

Wesley hangs his head in embarrassment.

T.J. waits for silence.

                  T.J.
We could have been friends all this time.

               WESLEY
Yes.

                  T.J.
I apologize, Wesley.

               WESLEY
It's okay.

                    T.J.
          It's not okay to hurt others just because
          the world hurts you.

                    WESLEY
          I shouldn't have said what I did.

                    T.J.
          Still want to be friends?

                    WESLEY
          Yes.

                    T.J.
          See? Now there's something that makes
          me happy.

T.J. hops down off the stage and runs up to Wesley and offers her hand in friendship. They shake on it. The audience breaks into vigorous applause.

EXT. INGERSOLL FRONT PORCH — DAY

Stephen sits on the top step, drinking coffee, waiting.

EXT. HARRY'S MAIL ROUTE — DAY

Harry approaches and stops when he sees Stephen on the steps.

                    STEPHEN
          You going to stand there all day, or do I
          get my mail?

It is a long march under such scrutiny.

STEPHEN
What's on your shoe?

Harry looks down at his shoes.

HARRY
The route is loaded with dogs.

STEPHEN
What are we going to do with you?

HARRY
Wouldn't mind a cup of coffee.

STEPHEN
I have no more coffee for you, Harry.
It's not how we operate here.

HARRY
I let myself down, too. It was all so
big...so new...loud. I'm used to a quiet
life.

STEPHEN
Greatest misjudgment of character I've
ever made. Outside of my own.

HARRY
I'm so miserable now. I'm lost.

STEPHEN
That my mail?

Harry hands him a handful of mail.

HARRY

I'm going to talk to her...try to explain.

Stephen gets up. Harry flinches.

STEPHEN

Wait here a minute.

Stephen goes inside. Harry waits, nervously.

FULL SCREEN

A headstone reads: MEGAN INGERSOLL

A single rose is placed in front of it.

REVEAL

EXT. TEXAS CEMETERY/GRAVESIDE — DAY

Kevin stands up, having just placed the rose.

KEVIN

I see now how I locked you out.

Megan embraces him from behind.

MEG

Not here.

KEVIN

I didn't know how to let you in.

MEG

Not yet.

                    KEVIN
        What I worked so hard to prevent I
        ended up creating.


                    MEG
        Shhh...

EXT. BICYCLE/MOVING — DAY

Her legs pumping like pistons, T.J. sails through an
empty intersection.

A PICKUP TRUCK approaches and turns in the same
direction as T.J.

Its vanity license plate reads: *A ROGUE.*


INT. DENTAL OFFICE — DAY

The Dentist is in the middle of drilling on a male patient.
Darlene is not attentive.

                    DENTIST
        Suction.

Darlene remains oblivious.

                    DENTIST
        Suction, please.

Darlene plunges the suction tube into the patient's
mouth. He gags and nearly comes out of the chair.

EXT. BICYCLE/MOVING — DAY

T.J. is on a mission.

A ROGUE glides along behind her.

EXT. INGERSOLL HOME — DAY

Stephen comes out of the house with all his UNIFORMS
and a bag of POLISHED SHOES.

Harry expected...perhaps a shotgun.

> STEPHEN
> Start looking professional.

> HARRY
> Your uniforms?

> STEPHEN
> You give Postal Carriers a bad name.

> HARRY
> You giving them to me?

> STEPHEN
> Too fine a breed for that.

> HARRY
> Your shoes too?

> STEPHEN
> I'm through hanging onto things I don't
> need anymore.

                    HARRY
Can I give you something for them?

                   STEPHEN
Better not stop in anymore, Harry. Not
the way things stand.

                    HARRY
      Yeah.

HARRY can't seem to get himself going.

                   STEPHEN
      Go on, now.

                    HARRY
      Right.

Like a beast struggling under burden, Harry turns and
goes. Stephen watches after him.

EXT. POST OFFICE — DAY

T.J. careens up to a bicycle rack in front, secures her
bicycle, and goes inside.

A ROGUE pulls into the lot and parks. We see that

CHESTER is behind the wheel.

INT. POST OFFICE — DAY

T.J. is next in line and steps up to the counter and
presents a letter.

                              T.J.
              First Class, please.

The Clerk tears a stamp off a sheet and reaches for
T.J.'s money with a smile.

SLOW MOTION/SILENCE

Before the exchange can be made, the clerk is hit by a
bullet in the middle of the forehead and sinks slowly out
of sight.

A spray of bullets rips up the wall behind the counter.

T.J. is slow to respond as she turns to see Chester
wielding an automatic assault rifle in broad sweeping
arcs across the Post Office.

Everyone has been caught by surprise as he makes sure
that every last individual goes down.

He takes out a hand gun, swallows the muzzle, and
fires.

Silence.

EXT. POST OFFICE/SILENCE — DAY

PULL BACK

As the building recedes it looks unremarkable. Two
vehicles drive by going in opposite directions.

                              T.J. (V.O.)
              Dear Uncle Kevin.

SOUND slowly filters back in as our retreat continues and banal evidence of life-as-usual is revealed: a pedestrian or two, a delivery being made, yard work being done, children playing, etc.

EXT. MUSTANG/MOVING — DAY

Stephen pulls into the School Parking Lot.

> T.J. (V.O.)
> Something happened.

INT. CLASSROOM — DAY

Barbara vigorously cleans the blackboard.

> T.J. (V.O.)
> The world has gone Postal.

Barbara is surprised by Stephen in the doorway.

> STEPHEN
> You keep a very nice room.

> BARBARA
> Everything has a place.

> STEPHEN
> I have never seen you teach.

> BARBARA
> You were always welcome.

> STEPHEN
> Let's take a drive?

> BARBARA
>
> I have my car.

> STEPHEN
>
> We'll come back for it.

> BARBARA
>
> Whenever you have bad news, we go for
> a ride so you won't have to look at me.

> STEPHEN
>
> What I lack in courage I make up for in
> predictability.

> BARBARA
>
> Are you going to leave me?

> STEPHEN
>
> No.

Barbara gets her jacket and they disappear down the corridor.

EXT. POST OFFICE FRONT DOOR — DAY

Movement is visible through the door.

T.J. backs out the door as if falling out of the building. Blood-smeared and terrified, she lurches toward her bicycle.

> T.J. (V.O)
>
> You've probably heard about the Post
> Office shooting here.

INT. SHOWER — DAY

T.J. stands under a steaming cascade of water.

She smears some blood between thumb and forefinger.

> T.J.
>
> Viscosity.

ON her feet, bloody water spools down the drain.

> T.J. (V.O.)
> I was the only survivor.

EXT. BACK OF DENTAL OFFICE — DAY

Darlene comes out and stops upon seeing Harry leaning against her car.

> DARLENE
> Get off my car.

> HARRY
> Can we talk?

> DARLENE
> Go home to your fishing show, your Cheetos, and your Paint By Numbers imagination.

> HARRY
> Ever do anything you were ashamed of and wish you could take it back?

DARLENE
You mean like loving you?

HARRY
I wish you'd let me explain.

DARLENE
I don't want to hear it.

Darlene gets into her car but makes no move to start
the engine.

Harry leans against the fender by the door; they remain
a continent apart.

They wait.

Darlene rolls down her window.

HARRY
I can't eat.

DARLENE
I have never felt pain like that before.

HARRY
Can't sleep.

DARLENE
Not even when Richard left.

HARRY
My best friend is through with me.

                    DARLENE
We were never friends.

                    HARRY
I meant your father.

                    DARLENE
Wish you knew what it felt like.

                    HARRY
Maybe that's the part we should work on.
Feelings.

                    DARLENE
Men have no feelings.

                    HARRY
Notice anything different about me?

Darlene looks closely at Harry.

                    DARLENE
You're odd, Harry. Very odd.

                    HARRY
New uniform. New shoes.

                    DARLENE
Look all right.

                    HARRY
Feel like a new man.

DARLENE
I never asked you to be anyone but who
you are.

HARRY
Think I could eat something if I had
congenial company.

DARLENE
I know you're not asking me to dinner.

HARRY
I told you right from the get-go I was
peculiar.

DARLENE
Because that would mean you're just
plain stupid.

HARRY
*Edna-Mae, that boy ain't right.*

DARLENE
There will be no more package deals in
Las Vegas.

HARRY
That is not any kind of a real place.

DARLENE
No rush. We take our time.

HARRY
Sounds good to me.

> DARLENE
> I want something to celebrate. And my
> family in attendance.

> HARRY
> I'd like that too.

> DARLENE
> You just going to sit out there on the
> fender of my car?

Harry jumps up, trots around to the passenger door and gets in.

After an awkward moment's delay, he and Darlene throw themselves into each other's arms.

EXT. MUSTANG/MOVING — DAY

Open prairie highway. The distant horizon is a straight line. The sky offers more variety than the landscape.

INT. MUSTANG/MOVING — DAY

Stephen and Barbara ride in silence.

> BARBARA
> Can't tell you what's going through my
> mind.

Stephen pulls off onto the shoulder and slides the gear selector into park. He looks at Barbara square in the eye.

STEPHEN
I was headed out of town.

BARBARA
Where are we going?

STEPHEN
The minute I heard *pregnant* I went
down and bought a bus ticket.

BARBARA
Where would you have gone?

STEPHEN
Out west. See the ocean.

BARBARA
Never wanted to be anyone's mother.

STEPHEN
My bags were packed.

BARBARA
All of a sudden I was desperate.

STEPHEN
Thought hard work could make up for it.

BARBARA
Out of my mind. I could not let you run
out on me.

STEPHEN
You knew?

                    BARBARA
Suspected.


                    STEPHEN
Landlocked my whole life.


                    BARBARA
I knew if I said *I'd take care of it* you
would stay. I'm not sure I ever even
wanted to get married. I was undone.


                    STEPHEN
I live in shame.


                    BARBARA
I threw away everything I thought I had
wanted for myself.

They turn away from each other and watch the horizon.

LATER — DUSK

The car continues to idle but has not moved.
They sit like statues, staring straight ahead.

MUCH LATER — NIGHT

They can see now only as far as the headlights will
allow.


                    BARBARA
I left a brand new pair of Spectators there
when we ran out. I wonder what the
person thought who found those shoes,
the sheet, that empty apartment?

                    STEPHEN
          Something happened here.

                    BARBARA
          Something sure did.

                    STEPHEN
          What do we do now?

                    BARBARA
          Let's go home.

Barbara caresses the side of Stephen's face. He savors her touch.

EXT. MUSTANG — NIGHT

They execute a U-turn and head back to town.

                    T.J. (V.O)
          Media people won't leave me alone.

EXT. INGERSOLL HOME — NIGHT

The Mustang pulls up to find the driveway and frontage crowded with police cruisers parked at differing angles, lights blazing, uniformed officers waiting on them.

                    T.J. (V.O.)
          I was on national television.

Stephen and Barbara abandon the car and run toward the house, where officers displaying T.J.'s backpack and her unstamped letter move toward them.

                    T.J. (V.O.)
          I'm on home-study for awhile because of
          all the reporters swarming around the
          school, our neighborhood.

EXT.  COASTAL HIGHWAY/MOVING — DAY

The Pacific Ocean is a world away from the landlocked
town of Springfield, Illinois.

FIND AND FOLLOW

A white rental sedan as it pulls off the highway into a
sandy dune area of beach

                    T.J. (V.O.)
          Mom and Gordon, alias Harry, are going
          to try to get married again. I like him.
          And I think we're all going to be very
          happy as a family.

The car comes to a stop with the Oregon vanity license
plate in view: *4 MEGAN.*

EXT. PARKING AREA/BEACH/WATER — DAY

Kevin, T.J., Stephen, and Barbara emerge from the car
and stand in awe of the vast Pacific Ocean.

                    T.J. (V.O.)
          We're going to let them have Springfield,
          while we get out of town. Here we come!

                    STEPHEN
          It's so much more.

Barbara takes Stephen's hand.

                    BARBARA
          Let's get wet.

They head down through the dunes onto the beach.

                    KEVIN
          What do you think?

                    T.J.
          Race you to the water.

T.J. takes off running toward the water's edge. Kevin
follows, but something makes him turn back.

High on a dune stands MEGAN. The full skirt of her
sundress blossoms in the breeze. She offers a last and
loving wave.

Kevin kicks off his shoes and runs full-tilt after T.J.
toward the white-capped surf.

FADE OUT

CPSIA information can be obtained at www.ICGtesting.com
Printed in the USA
BVOW000042160513

320836BV00002B/2/P